C000177248

1 MONTH OF
FREE
READING

at

www.ForgottenBooks.com

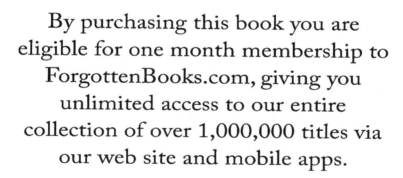

By purchasing this book you are eligible for one month membership to ForgottenBooks.com, giving you unlimited access to our entire collection of over 1,000,000 titles via our web site and mobile apps.

To claim your free month visit: www.forgottenbooks.com/free830552

ISBN 978-0-483-97212-4
PIBN 10830552

Historic, archived document

Do not assume content reflects current
scientific knowledge, policies, or practices.

The Eastern Poultryman.

ESTABLISHED 1899 AS THE POULTRYMAN AND POMOLOGIST.
DEVOTED TO PRACTICAL POULTRY CULTURE.

| Vol. 3. | South Freeport, Maine, October, 1901. | No 2. |

ROSE COMB BROWN LEGHORNS.

The Eastern Poultryman.

ESTABLISHED 1899 AS THE POULTRYMAN AND POMOLOGIST.

DEVOTED TO PRACTICAL POULTRY CULTURE.

| Vol. 3. | South Freeport, Maine, October, 1901. | No 2. |

Successes and Failures in Poultry Keeping.

Written for the Eastern Poultryman.

There are two ways of raising poultry, the right and the wrong way; the right way leads to success, the wrong way to failure.

To illustrate I will give the readers of the *Eastern Poultryman* a true account of a visit I made to two young friends of mine not long since.

. Both were well situated, having good buildings and unlimited range; both living on farms, both started at the same (spring of 1898), both had money to do with, both were young and great workers. As I do not wish to give names I will call one Mr. A, the other Mr. B.

I visited Mr. A last August. His place is on a high hill, with neighbors not near enough to bother. The land is rocky, but good, rich grass land. His hen house is built of matched boards, shingled roof, sides, ends and front covered with tar paper. This house is built on the scratching shed plan, two hundred feet long, twenty-five feet wide, eight feet high in front, four feet at back, making an ideal house for 300 fowls. He had large, roomy yards, but with the exception of two small plum trees not a vestige of shade. The house was provided with twenty windows and faced the south, the windows being all on the north side.

Scattered all around were brooders and brooding houses in abundance. Everything showed that money had been invested lavishly. His wife told me that he had two good Prairie State Incubators, one 300 and one 300 egg capacity.

Mr. A was away at the time of my arrival I found his wife very much disgusted and discouraged with the poultry business; she declared "it didn't pay and that if they got a dollar out of hens they had to put it right back into houses, coops, brooders or feed; and there is always some trouble with fowls, sick or dying, or eggs not hatching." "Why," said she, "commencing January 1st we have set 3,000 eggs and only about 1,000 chickens hatched out; not half our eggs were fertile; the chicks have been dying mostly from being stuck up (diarrhœa) until we have left about 400 and they are still dying. There is no money in it and I am sure my husband does all he can. I wish he would quit the business." About this time her husband drove into the yard with a load of dry goods boxes and pointing at them his wife said; "There, he has taken to save a lot of eggs and brings back dry goods boxes to make some more coops and so it goes."

After dinner Mr. A invited me to look over his plant. I saw he hesitated and finally informed me that he had been very busy haying and had not had time to clean up, having left the hens for his father, an old man, to care for, but said he frankly, "things don't go as smoothly as I would like. If you can tell me where the trouble lies I would feel grateful."

We first went to look at his chickens, and to feed them he took two pails of soft food, corn and oats ground. Taking some of this food in my hand I found it was cold and sloppy; smelling of it I found it was sour. I asked him how long it had been wet up, and he informed me that his wife wet it up in the morning so as to let it swell. He then told me that to save time he fed whole wheat mornings, soft food at noon and cracked corn at night.

I found about 400 chickens of all sizes running together and from three to five months of age. He fed in long wooden troughs which were filthy and sour, and when the food was put into the trough the larger chickens crowded and trampled over the smaller ones and we found six dead chicks lying around the yard.

Lifting up the brooder covers I found them covered with about one inch of chick manure. Looking into his brooder houses I found them ill-smelling and filthy, and brooders and brooder houses were very lousy. I should think they had not been cleaned during the whole season.

Going from the chickens to the hen house I noticed that the yards were baked down hard so that there was no chance for the fowls to dig or dent. Digging up a small piece of one yard with a spade it came up in great chunks, and there were places where the top looked green and slimy. The inside of his hen house had never seen any whitewash, but he informed me that he cleaned it out once a month, using coal oil on his roosts. His nests were built under his dropping boards. Before we had gone half way through his hen house I felt lice crawling over me.

His stock consisted of White Leghorns and White Wyandottes. The White Wyandottes were over-fat, the posterior of many being bare, hanging down and looking red and inflamed. The necks and breasts of some were bare of feathers and the crops of many looked red and swollen. This he informed me was the stock from which he had been breeding. The males were inferior, under sized and scrubby looking, and the wonder to me was that he had been able to hatch one thousand chicks from three thousand eggs, and that he had saved even four hundred chicks out of the one thousand.

Coming out of the hen house I saw seven hens which had lost the use of their legs. (Paralysis of the legs.) I asked him why he did not kill them, and he informed me that they laid most every day and he thought they would get well.

We went to the house, and his wife soon joined us and asked me what I thought of the chicken business as conducted by her husband.

I frankly told her that I did not think much of it. She asked, "How can we better it; what would you advise?"

I advised them to change the method of feeding; to feed soft food in the morning and to feed it sweet and not sloppy, using only water enough to make it crumbly and to salt it just a little. I told them that shorts, meal and gluten mixed with ground oats in equal parts was better for a morning mash than ground corn and oats. I advised them to use for a noon feed rye, barley, wheat and oats, giving rye one day, barley the next, wheat the next, oats the next, and so on, and at night giving cracked corn to chicks and whole corn to old fowl, and to be sure to give enough and no more.

I suggested burning all the pails and wooden dishes he had been using for water; to scald and clean his feeding troughs ; to whitewash the inside of brooders, brooder houses and hen house, and to use some good liquid lice killer on roosts and dropping boards. I advised him to water his fowls and chicks three times daily; to separate his chickens, keeping the small ones by themselves; to keep oyster shells and grit by hens and chicks all the time; to purchase a good bone cutter and give fowls and chicks green bone three times per week; to build yards behind his hen house, so as to have two yards for each pen. Then he could sow down one yard and after it was up about six inches he could turn his fowls in and sow down the others. By this means he could supply his breeders with green food all the time. I advised him to sell all his old stock and purchase two good thrifty pens for next season's breeders, as I did not think that he would have any stock fit to breed from. His wife asked me if I did not think some of his pullets would do if he should purchase new males. I told her the stock would very likely be stunted and unfit to use as breeders, but that perhaps some of them, taking the very best, would answer for layers, but on no account would I use any of the fowls or chicks he then had for breeding.

I advised him to remove his nests from under his dropping boards, as they were hard to keep clean, and made good lice nests.

I suggested removing about two inches of the earth floor from his hen house and the hauling in of good dry sand to fill up; told him his dropping boards should be cleaned off twice a week at the least, and his brooders and brooder houses should be kept sweet and clean. I advised him to kill and bury deep all sick chickens, including the seven hens which had lost the use of their legs; to disinfect his brooders and brooder houses by burning sulphur in them, and to do the same in the roosting rooms in his hen house.

I told him I had found some of the prepared foods very good, and advised him to try them, as they were all ready to feed and very convenient. I told him I had fed these foods two years from the shell to the hatchet with good results. After I had finished, his wife asked me why I advised him to purchase pure stock, and inquired if I did not consider the common fowls to be just as good and to cost less.

"Well," said I, "for comparison, suppose we compare the White Wyandottes with your dunghills. Your dunghills will not lay any better and for poultry will not make as good an appearance; some of them will have blue, some black, some white, and some yellow legs. Their eggs will be small, medium and large, and the fowls will be of all sizes and colors, and will not stand neglect any better than pure breeds.

The White Wyandottes will, if well bred, lay an even colored egg of good size and when placed on the market will all look alike, making a uniform appearance, more pleasing to the eye of the purchaser, and the flesh is finer with a better appearance.

She admitted that this was true, but said she "do you think the White Wyandottes the best breed for eggs and poultry?" I told her I was not a White Wyandotte breeder but believed them to be a good general purpose fowl, and that I believed the best fowl had not yet been discovered; that each breeder was very likely to think the variety he bred the best, but for her husband's business, namely : eggs and poultry for market, the White Wyandotte, considering his locality and market was perhaps as good as any, but that he must be very careful and purchase only fine, vigorous stock and be sure that his males were not related to his females ; and I would by all means place shade in his breeding yards, which he could do by setting out some pine trees for immediate benefit ; at the same time I advised setting pear or plum trees for permanent shade, and he could remove the pines as soon as the fruit trees grew large enough to furnish shade.

When leaving, his wife asked me if I honestly believed poultry paid. I told her that I had been breeding poultry since 1872 and had found it paid me, but that it would not bear neglect and said I, "I don't know any business that will bear neglect, do you?" Both she and her husband admitted that this was true. I left them and have since heard that Mr. A. was making radical improvements which certainly were greatly needed.

About the last of August I paid a long promised visit to Mr. B. Mr. B. started at the same time as did Mr. A. (spring of 1898) and is to-day one of the most successful poultrymen in the state, and in my next I will tell you about that visit, which was certainly one of the most instructive visits I ever made to a poultryman.

The trouble with Mr. A. seems to be that he did real well the first year, making a profit, as he informed me, of $500. His buildings were new, stock clean and good, but later he grew careless, lice and overfeed, impure water, want of shade, want of judgment in selecting and mating breeding stock, allowing chicks of all ages and sizes to run together, leaving dead chicks lying around, letting sick fowls and chicks run with the flocks, in fact, breeding in a "don't care" sort of a way ; all of the above had nearly ruined him. But there is a chance for him to recover.

J. W. MORSE.

EPPING, N. H.

Rhode Island Red Enthusiast.

Written for the Eastern Poultryman.

Recently the writer spent a few hours pleasantly with Harry C. Nunan, who is for the present located at Cape Porpoise and is devoting a part of his time to breeding pure bred poultry. Mr. Nunan was formerly a salesman in Massachusetts, but finding his health was not all that could be desired, resulting from work largely indoors, he last fall changed his occupation and moved to Maine to engage in out-of-door pursuits.

Mr. Nunan commenced breeding S. C. White Leghorns several years ago and soon after took up the breeding of S. C. Rhode Island Reds. At Lynn in 1900 his Leghorns were among the 1st prize winners, receiving high scores. Has raised birds scoring as high as 94 points. Mr. Nunan believes in starting with the best stock one can buy and breeding his own show birds from it. He is very careful to know the breeding of his birds and by knowing the pedigree of the chicks from the choicest birds he can mate his hens with males of his own breeding and not inbreed too closely, and knowing their breeding he doesn't make the haphazard matings that breeders often do who buy their males from different strains which practice often results disastrously. By breeding in line Mr. N. keeps his flocks improving each year and buys but few birds. He believes in having the breeding stock together some time before the hatching season, and often mates his hens in December. Mr. N. is a strong believer in the practical side of poultry culture, but in his matings many a bird that would breed good practical stock is neglected and their places filled by better colored specimens.

As a money-making breed, Mr. N. thinks it very difficult to find an equal of the Rhode Island Red. He is raising mostly Rhode Island Reds and predicts a brilliant future for them.

Where Mr. Nunan is located seems to be an excellent place for rearing medium, early and late chicks, they having a greater variety of range and natural food than chicks usually get. A creek borders the land on one side, and the birds get small fish, etc., that the tide leaves on the beach, also plenty of shells within reach at all times, and when the small beach or seashore becomes too hot there is a large grove of oak trees near by for shade. Nearby cottages and hotels insure a good market for the poultry products during the summer.

Mr. N.'s advice to those just starting in the poultry business is to begin small and learn the business thoroughly, then increase the stock as fast as house room is enlarged and no faster. He believes in advertising and says he gets benefit from it in after years. He made egg sales last spring from an ad that appeared three years ago in a certain publication. He spoke highly of the POULTRYMAN as a practical paper, also as an advertising medium. He thinks the coming show in December is going to be of great benefit to the breeders of the Pine Tree state.

E. T. PERKINS.

The Origin of the Brown Egg Fad.

(Written for the Eastern Poultryman.)

While the white shelled egg is still preferred in some sections the brown shelled egg is ultra-fashionable in New England and throughout the greater part of the country.

Perfectly fresh eggs, laid by healthy hens that are fed the same kinds of food will taste precisely the same be their shells white or brown.

The brown shelled eggs are laid by hens that recrete coloring matter or pigment in that portion of the oviduct where the shell is completed.

Hens whose animal economy does not furnish this colored pigment lay white shelled eggs.

Let us examine a chocolate colored shell laid by a Plymouth Rock of a "brown egg strain." We find that the color does not permeate the entire shell. The inner membrane that first encloses the egg before the shell is formed is white; the structure of the shell itself is white; the outer surface of the shell only is brown. It is merely a surface tint from the brush of the artist Nature serving to distinguish one family from another. Who can say that birds in their wild state are not guided and aided in the protection of their species by the color of their eggs?

It is said that the color of the flower serves to point out to the bees the place where honey is to be found and the bee in turn carries the life-giving pollen to other flowers.

The brown color of the egg shell being confined to the outer surface cannot effect the flavor of the egg; but there can be no doubt that many people have had and do have the idea that brown shelled eggs are better than white shelled eggs. There is a reason for everything (even for the man who, having no brains of his own, steals the ideas of others) and there must be a reason for this. Brown shelled eggs formerly denoted that the hens that produced them were Asiatics or had Asiatic blood. The Asiatic breeds lay large eggs. Is it not true that years ago when the "brown egg fad" began to be noticed that the brown shelled eggs in our city markets were generally larger than those having white shells? If so, the people would naturally prefer them.

But there was another condition twenty-five or thirty years ago that it seems reasonable to suppose might have had a tendency to bring the white egg into discredit and thus boom the brown egg. That was the practice of pickling and liming eggs to preserve them; a practice that is still followed but not so extensively since the advent of cold storage. A pickled or a limed egg is not a very delectable article of diet as every good housewife knows. The brown shelled blood (Asiatic) was not so common on our farms then as now. The greater part of the eggs picked up by the country collectors for preserving were white shelled, hence the ill-tasting preserved egg was more commonly white than brown.

The writer remembers an egg merchant who did a considerable business "preserving" eggs for the Boston market and it was said that he experimented not a little to find a way to color the pickled eggs a brown that would have a natural appearance, but without success.

Is it not reasonable then to infer that the "brown egg fad" had a logical basis?

Brown eggs were generally good eggs, white eggs were frequently of inferior flavor as preserved eggs always have been and probably always will be.

Public opinion is not easily changed. A market that once demanded a brown egg for good reasons would continue to demand it after those reasons had disappeared unless some condition should arise to warrant a change.

So while we know that there is no difference in the eating qualities of white and brown shelled eggs, and that as far as beauty goes the color or absence of color on the shell is a matter of individual opinion, we must give the market what it most desires, be it brown shelled or white shelled eggs.

F. O. WELLCOME,
Yarmouth, Me.

A Word for the Light Brahmas.

For thirty-five years I have bred the Light Brahma, and still love them above all other breeds. Experience has taught me that first impressions upon the young mind are the ones that make a lasting impression, and mould the destiny of that character. To fulfill the desires that impression has made, one will undergo the privations and vicissitudes of a lifetime. This we can see in all walks of life: men and women striving to fulfill the destiny that a first impression has made.

When I was a small boy, away back in the '50's, my mother took me with her to visit a neighbor who had quite a large flock of Light Brahmas. I remember it, as distinctly as yesterday, how interested I was in watching the hens, noting how large they were and comparing them to turkeys. The hens completely filled the nests, and such big nests, too. They promised me that if I was a good boy all day I might help gather the eggs in the evening. So you may know with what anxiety I waited for the time to gather the eggs. When it came, I held in my hands the largest and finest eggs I had ever seen. I exacted a promise from my mother that she would buy some of those fine chickens, which she did before she went home.

This is where and how I received my first impression of the Light Brahma, and as I grew older this fine breed grew more beautiful to my eye. My ambition, from the first, was to have good birds; and while I do not claim to have better birds than any one else, I do claim to have good ones. I have never seen the day that I regretted taking up the Light Brahma, although I have made mistakes and changed my mode of caring for and feeding them. Through it all I did not say "quit," but shut my teeth and made greater effort towards perfection. When I look back over the rough road I have travelled in my breeding, feeding, and rearing of chickens, I wonder that I did not fall by the wayside. Those who stay are the ones who win in the end. Those who go in with a rush, fall down and quit, are the ones that help to keep the stayer to the sticking point. We have stayers in this world of ours; men who have spent almost a lifetime breeding the all-round good chicken—the Light Brahma—they swear that they are the money-makers. They have stood the test of time and improvement; there is no other breed of fowls that has survived the amount of. abuse, mismanagement and over-indulgence on the part of breeders. The Light Brahma is still with us and as ever ready, if properly bred and cared for, to make more money for their owners than any other chicken. But people go by fads in this world; and almost all breeds have created a fad, as those who have watched the poultry business know, and we have some fads now; but the old Light Brahma is making the money for the ones who have stuck to them the same as usual.

Every one who undertakes to breed poultry must study the requirements of the business, besides the individual requirements of each particular breed, or they will never make a success. I am satisfied, from what I have learned from my experience (as I have handled some other breeds besides Light Brahmas), that they all require a certain line of management peculiarly their own. In other words, to make the most out of any breed, you must know how to develop their best points to the highest degree of perfection. If you would make a success of breeding and raising chickens, it behooves you to know why you are doing a thing and how you are doing it; and it is only by using brains that you will attain any degree of proficiency. I have raised chickens for years; I won't say I bred them, for I can look back and see that at one time I did not know how to breed. Before I knew much about them I was raising them for my own pleasure and what profit I could get out of them as market poultry, and the Light Brahma has always stood first. In the course of time, people began to comment upon my birds, and want to swap eggs (oh yes! I have passed through that ordeal), and I began to wonder if there was not a way and chance to improve. For the first four years that I began to improve my flock, I found hard work and worse dis-appointment. I talked with the best judges and breeders in the country; went to poultry shows; got up shows and superintended shows on purpose to learn; but all this time I did not show a bird, although I had some of them run over by some of the best judges in the country. This I did to find out how much improvement I was making, and if my judgment in mating was proving worthy or not, and I did not advertise eggs or birds for sale although I had birds scoring from 90 to 94, because I wanted to know for a certainty that my birds would breed on. I have learned from experience how to feed, manage and breed the Light Brahma, and my business has had a good steady, healthy growth, as I have customers that have bought from me for eight years, and if I have a dissatisfied customer he has kept his mouth shut.

The Light Brahma has held its shape better than any other breed, taking into consideration the length of time they have been with us, although there have too much Cochin shape to suit me. Not all breeders, however have made this mistake; otherwise, the shape has been improved in most respects as well as color in the last thirty-five years. As in other breeds, standard color is the hardest item to control. Some breeders have neglected shape, and still have straw color on the backs; but to take the Light Brahma on the whole, there has been vast improvement, and we breeders of them have nothing to be ashamed of. This does not mean that we can get careless, but we must watch every section and breed out every defect, or rather, breed as near the Standard as possible, as that is our guide. Study your birds and breed to improve them, applies to all breeds as well as the Light Brahma.

Depend upon yourself. It is well enough to get all the information possible and that is essential; but you might sit for forty-eight hours and listen to the different methods of mating, managing and breeding, and only remember a small per cent of what you have heard. These things have been talked over, written and preached about, but mortals are forgetful, and for that reason have to be reminded often, so as to urge them to gain part of their knowledge by experience.

The Light Brahma to-day and that of thirty-five years ago are the same general type, and for health and hardiness they stand out in bold relief as the peer of the chicken kingdom, for they have stood the test of time, the supreme leveler. They have been bumped around by other breeds, cried down and scoffed at; but when it comes to the business of making money they will make more to the square inch than most people would suppose. They are stayers, and are here to stay. What more do we need?—*Golden Egg.*

Start Right.

A person who desires to adopt some profession or trade as a means of earning a livelihood must necessarily spend some time in preparation before he can hope to begin business for himself. How long do you suppose a person would be able to carry on a successful dry goods or grocery business, should he attempt to conduct such business without any previous experience whatever? He would undoubtedly fail before the first year had passed.

Why, then, should any one expect to succeed in the breeding of standard bred poultry without any previous experience or knowledge of the breeds.

Many persons who are fairly successful in the ordinary business of life, will make a decided failure in the poultry business simply through ignorance. In many cases they have never seen nor heard of the standard of perfection, and have not the slightest knowledge of the standard requirements of the breed they have adopted. We heard of a breeder (?) of Light Brahmas, who discarded several of his hens because they had black feathers in their wings.

The highly colored, fancy sketches, of little work and big profits, connected with the breeding of standard poultry, that appear from time to time in many of our poultry journals, tempt many a person to invest their money in a business of the first requirements of which they are densely ignorant. There is money to be made in poultry breeding, but it will be made by those who have given the matter careful study, thus gaining a knowledge of the requirements of their variety, and who will mate intelligently to produce the desired points.

To beginners we would say invest the first dollar of your capital in a copy of the *American Standard of Perfection,* study the requirements of the breed you fancy, then buy stock of some well known breeder and have him mate them for you.

Do not expect to get birds that will exactly fit the standard description, for that kind of stock has never yet been produced, but get good stock if only a few in number.

Don't get the idea into your head that you know all there is to know but rather try and learn a little every day. Never make a mating without having some object in view, and be able to tell why you mated in that way to produce the required points.

In other words give to your poultry culture the same careful thought and intelligent study that you would to any other business that you desired to enter and success will be yours.

In order to establish a paying business extra good stock is required and in order to produce this quality of stock the breeder must possess patience, brains and a willingness to learn from others.—*Kentucky Poultry Journal.*

The best flavored eggs come from feeding the hen with carbonaceous foods; the poorest, from highly nitrogenous. Grains and clover yield the best flavor.

DANGER FOR RHODE ISLAND REDS.

Utility Qualities Are Widely Appreciated, but Serious Faults May Shelve Them as a Pure Breed. An Ideal Standard the Only Remedy.

Fanciers and breeders admit the rapidly increasing interest in Rhode Island Reds during the past few years, not only among farmers, but among breeders of choice stock, especially in the eastern and middle states. They have won their way on their merits as an all-purpose fowl. Their attractive appearance also adds very much to their chance of becoming very popular in every section of the country. Their good qualities are now pretty well understood, and they hold a secure place as producers of large tinted eggs, as desirable dressed poultry. As pure-bred fowls, however, they are not in good standing. Their lack of uniformity in breeding, both as regards type and color, has seriously hindered their general introduction among fanciers. Although these faults do not lessen their popularity among farmers and market producers, they do make them less satisfactory in other quarters. The millions who have kept the carefully bred varieties that are so common to-day will not be satisfied with mongrel breeders. Any stock that will not breed a fairly uniform looking flock, no matter how good for business, will have no permanent place in their yards.

TOO MANY TYPES, COLORS, AND QUALITIES.

Egg producers who originated and perpetuated Reds followed none of the fancier's methods. They were satisfied that the Reds should remain mongrel breeders, provided they were prime egg producers and made good dressed poultry. Hardly any two producers bred them alike in shape or size, neither did they carefully select specimens to establish any particular color. Their size would go up one season and down the next, and their shape and color would change, also, according to the lot of males secured to breed from each season. This condition of things existed twenty or more years ago, and continues to-day among the large egg farmers. A few of the males produced are an attractive bright red, but more are not. The hens come all colors, from dark brown to straw color, and usually all are saved and bred from. Such stock can be found by hundreds and thousands on most of the farms within fifteen or twenty miles of where Rhode Island Reds originated. There are millions of them in existence within that area. The producer who wants just egg-layers or dressed poultry stock, and expects nothing like a pure breed, makes no mistake in getting such, because he can buy it very cheap. Its behavior will not disappoint him. He can find small, quick-maturing specimens or larger and hardier birds as he prefers; also those of many different shapes. All, although crude low-grade stock, are real Rhode Island Reds. Twenty or more years of breeding to no particular type, color or kind of comb leaves them mongrels still.

THE IMPROVED REDS.

In great contrast to this stock are the modern improved Reds. Years ago a few fanciers commenced to breed carefully selected specimens, endeavoring to produce a creditable pure breed. The use of some of this material to produce two new buff breeds was what called special attention to the original stock. In some sections, farmers had preferred single combs on their birds and they were most common. In other neighborhoods, the use of rose comb males was favored, but the majority of flocks contained both kinds, and were bred together. The nearest buff specimens having each kind of comb had been introduced as a novelty, and eventually became known as Buff Plymouth Rocks and Buff Wyandottes. The call for this buff material and later for real Rhode Island Reds became quite brisk. A single-comb variety of Reds, with the natural markings of the original stock, was soon established that bred quite uniform and true to comb, and was exhibited at fairs and gained great favor. The demand for this stock was so great that, to meet it, anything and everything that would pass, regardless of its ancestry, was sold. When there was such a demand for Buff Wyandotte and Buff Plymouth Rock material, a great effort was made to breed out the black in tail and wing flights of both sexes and the black in hackles of females, which were natural characteristics of Rhode Island Reds. To get the even buff color, the natural contrast in color between the upper and lower portion of the body as usually found in both male and female Reds was also objectionable, and an even color from head to foot was sought. This stock bred to Buff Wyandotte and Buff Plymouth Rock Standard would throw some very nice dark red birds, having less contrast in color between neck, breast and back than was natural; also females with hackles free from black and with but little black in tail. From these a strain of Reds was established having a tendency to breed females without black in hackle. Under this arrangement, one pen would produce what could be sold as Buff Plymouth Rocks, Buff Wyandottes, and Single Comb, and Rose Comb Rhode Island Reds. No doubt the improved Reds produced in this way might be more refined in head, comb and earlobes than the crude Reds and have better undercolor, but they would breed a large number of buff males and females. After the demand for buff material subsided, and the popularity of Rhode Island Reds grew, what had been sold as Buffs were then sold as Reds.

BREEDING SEVERAL VARIETIES.

The improved Single Comb variety had been pretty well perfected, so it would approach a pure breed, before Rose Comb specimens were taken up by fanciers and bred and improved in the same direction, and they were considerably in advance of the latter in color and quality. Now some fanciers are working to perfect, from sports from Light Brahma ancestry, a Pea Comb variety, but it does not breed very well at present. Although the breeding of two or more varieties distinct only in having different combs is condemned by some former makers of the A. P. A. Standard, and especially by breeders of the new buff and other breeds, who would like to see them have but one comb, and that a pea comb, Rhode Island Red breeders themselves are not worried over the matter, and continue to breed the several varieties. If the sports from eachvariety are not sold or bred from regardless of ancestry, if they are bred as distinct varieties should be, I can see no objection to it; otherwise care-

fully bred flocks will be greatly injured.

THE DIFFERENCE IN QUALITY.

It should be distinctly understood that there is almost as much difference in quality in breeding between the crude egg-farm stock and the modern improved Reds, as now bred by many fanciers, as there is between the breeding of common mixed fowls and the best Plymouth Rocks and Wyandottes of to-day. As one class of Reds is plentiful and the well-bred stock is scarce, twenty or one hundred crude Reds can be, and probably are, sold to one improved specimen. There is no reason to regret this, provided they are sold for what they are and the buyer gets what he expects. The more unimproved Reds are scattered over the country, provided their owners understand their quality, the better for all concerned. But every mongrel specimen sent out, unless sold for what it is, hurts the improved stock in the eyes of the fancier and breeder of pure-bred stock, no matter how well it suits the market producer. Fanciers are very likely to think, if a long price is paid, that there are none better, and that they are so far away from a pure breed they will let them alone. Therefore, while meat and egg stock is being widely distributed and favorably known, those nearly like a pure breed are not rapidly advancing among the fanciers and careful breeders. Not until Reds are improved and refined so they will have a distinct shape of their own, breed a fairly uniform color, and each variety breed as true to comb as other varieties, will they rank with other pure breeds. If this is not done, they will fast lose ground among all but market producers. Nothing, but an ideal standard that is definite and exact will bring this about. It is for the interest of all breeders of high-class Reds that a standard shall be adopted that will enable any one to distinguish high-class from low-grade birds. Such a standard would protect both breeder and buyer. The breeder of choice stock would secure better prices, and all breeders would be induced to improve their stock. In no case would such a standard prevent the sale of unimproved meat and egg stock for what it is. It would interfere and work hardship only upon those who, either ignorantly or intentionally, sell mixed Reds for carefully-bred specimens and thus hinder their advancement as a pure breed.

CALL FOR VERY DARK BIRDS.

During the improvement of the Reds, fanciers have differed in their views as to the best type and color to work for. The new Buff Rock and Wyandotte standard has influenced their work altogether too much. As the new buff breeds came pretty red for some time, it was considered best to breed the real Reds darker than they naturally were, to make them dissimiliar. Other reasons have made the tendency to change their color very strong. One has been due to a misunderstanding on the part of buyers as to what the real color of a Rhode Island Red male and female should be. When Reds of the natural color were sent into other sections, the buyer, judging from the name, expected to receive Red females that matched the males, while the females are naturally reddish yellow or buff. Disappointed buyers, who had been sold buff stock, or who thought their genuine females not of the right color, called for very dark males to

(Continued on Page 27.)

Poultry at the Maine State Fair.

The exhibition of poultry at the State Fair this year was superior in quality to what is usually shown there, and contained a large number of birds that will make their marks in the winter shows. The breeders all over the state are looking forward to the exhibition of the Maine State Poultry and Pet Stock Association, at Lewiston in December, and many of them have been planning their work this season with that in mind. As a consequence we expected to see some good fowls and promising chicks—and they were there, while a few of the exhibitors are evidently keeping their chicks until December before showing.

The State Fair management still clings to the antediluvian method of pair entries. There is no particular reason for this, but as Noah established the custom, it has been followed by most of the fall fairs. The State Fair also needs a new building for poultry. In some parts of the building it was impossible to distinguish a buff fowl from a black, and the judge was obliged to take the birds one at a time to the windows in the end of the building. As the visitors were not expected to handle the birds, the exhibition failed of that one great purpose of live stock shows, viz., the education of the masses, as to true types and colors. Another glaring fault in the manner in which this show was managed was in not having the coops kept clean. Birds in the show pens should receive better care. The feeding and watering are important features and should never be slighted, and it is almost as important to have the coops cleaned each day and new litter added, and a little of some disinfectant would not come amiss. Even if there are no noxious germs in the air there are disagreeable odors that can be checked by the use of a good disinfectant.

It is time that a society like the State Fair Association should get out of the ruts and keep up with the times in its poultry department, as it does in some of its others, and the poultrymen themselves should make a firm request for better conditions.

The judging was by Mr. A. C. Hawkins, of Lancaster, Mass., who gave general satisfaction, placing the premiums as follows:—

Barred Plymouth Rocks—E. P Atwood, Auburn, 1st on fowl; F. S. Dearborn, Bangor, 2d on fowl; Parker & Scripture, Bangor, 2d on chicks; Daniel Stewart, Richmond, 3d on fowl, 3d on chicks; J. W. Lowell, Gardiner, 3d on chicks.

White Plymouth Rocks—Parke Dingley, Lewiston, 2d and 3d on fowl; F. A. Blaisdell, Monmouth, 3d on fowl, 1st and 2d on chicks; A. J. Kenniston, 1st ou fowl.

Buff Plymouth Rocks—I. V. McKenney, West Auburn, 1st and 2d on chicks; C. P. Swift, 1st and 2d on fowl; T. M. Lombard, Auburn, 2d on fowl and 3d on chicks.

American Dominiques—A. J. Kenniston, 1st and 2d on fowl, 1st, 2d and 3d on chicks.

White Wyandottes—Mrs. C. L. Cushman, Auburn, 1st and 2d on fowls; A. L. Merrill, Auburn, 1st on chicks; Nathan C. True, Litchfield, 3d on chicks; J. W. Lowell, 2d on fowl; A. J. Kenniston, 3d on fowl.

Buff Wyandottes—A. L. Merrill, Auburn, 1st, 2d and 3d on chicks, 3d on fowl; Frank S. Winslow, Freeport, 2d on fowl; E. A. Drinkwater, Sabattus, 1st on fowl.

Golden Wyandotte—Beulah Bartlett, Lewiston, 1st, 2d and 3d on fowl, 1st and 2d on chicks.

White Wonders—A. L. Merrill, 1st and 2d on fowl, 1st and 3d on chicks.

Buff Wonders—C. P. Swift, Wayne, 1st and 2d on fowl, 1st 2d and 3d on chicks.

Mottled Javas—E. A. Drinkwater, 1st on fowl and 1st on chicks.

Silver Wyandotte—Beulah Bartlett, 1st, 2d and 3d on fowl, 1st, 2d and 3d on chicks.

Light Brahmas—Charles L. Cushman, Auburn, 1st and 2d on fowl, 1st, 2d and 3d on chicks; Jas. L. Jordan, Sabattus, 3d on fowl.

Dark Brahmas—E. A. Drinkwater, 1st on fowl and chicks; S. Ward, 2d and 3d on fowl.

Buff Cochin—M. F. Burnham, Auburn, 1st on fowl; Parker & Scripture, 1st on chicks, 2d on fowl; E. A. Drinkwater, 2d on chicks, 3d on fowl; M. F. Burnham, 3d on chicks.

Partridge Cochin—E. A. Drinkwater, 1st on fowl; S. Ward, 2d on fowl.

White Cochins—S. Ward, 1st on fowl; E. A. Drinkwater, 1st on chicks and 2d on fowl.

Black Cochins—E. A. Drinkwater, 1st on fowl.

White Langshans—Geo. P. Coffin, So. Freeport, 1st and 2d on fowl.

Black Langshans—Geo. P. Coffin, 1st and 2d on fowl.

White Dorkings—A. J. Kenniston, 1st on fowl and chicks, 2d on chicks.

Silver Gray Dorkings—E. A. Drinkwater, 1st and 2d on chicks, 2d on fowl; A. J. Kenniston, 1st on fowl.

Colored Dorkings—A. J. Kenniston, 1st and 2d on fowl, 1st and 2d on chicks.

Silver Spangled Hamburgs—Frank E. Carville, Lewiston, 1st on chicks; E. A. Drinkwater, 1st on fowl and 2d on chicks; Parker & Scripture, 2d on fowl; Manley F. Burnham, 3d on fowl.

Silver Penciled Hamburgs— E. A. Drinkwater, 1st on fowl and chicks.

Golden Penciled—A. J. Kenniston, 1st and 2d on fowl.

Rhode Island Reds—E. T. Perkins, Saco, 1st on chicks.

Blue Andalusians—E. A. Drinkwater, 1st and 3d on fowl; S. Ward, 2d on fowl.

Red Caps—E. A. Drinkwater, 1st and 2d on fowl, 1st and 2d on chicks.

Black Minorcas—Parker & Scripture, 1st and 3d on fowl, 1st and 2d on chicks; E. A. Drinkwater, 2d on fowl.

Spanish—White Faced Black, E. A. Drinkwater, 1st on fowl and chicks.

Single Comb White Leghorn—Parker & Scripture, 1st on fowl, 2d on chicks; F. S. Dearborn, 3d on fowl; M. F. Burnham, 1st and 2d on chicks; F. H. Briggs, Auburn, 2d on fowl.

Rose Comb White Leghorn—Parker & Scripture, 1st on fowl, 1st and 3d on chicks; S. Ward, Richmond Corner, 2d on chicks.

Brown Leghorns—Single Comb, J. L. Jordan, 1st and 2d on chicks, 2d on fowl; Parker & Scripture, 3d on fowl; E. A. Drinkwater, 3d on chicks; A. J. Kenniston, 1st on fowl; Rose Comb, J. W. Lowell, 1st on fowl, 1st and 2d on chicks; Manley F. Burnham, 3d on fowl; Parker & Scripture, 2d on fowl, 3d on chicks.

Black Leghorn—Parker & Scripture, 1st on fowl; E. A. Drinkwater, 1st on chicks, 2d on fowl.

Buff Leghorns—E. T. Perkins, 1st on fowl, 1st and 3d on chicks; C. P. Swift, Wayne, 1st and 3d on chicks, 2d on fowl; M. F. Burnham, 3d on fowl.

Black Javas—A. J. Kenniston, 1st and 2d on chicks.

Houdans—F. M. Cummings, Lewiston, 3d on fowl, 1st, 2d and 3d on chicks; M. F. Burnham, 1st and 2d on fowl.

Sherwoods—Herman Corbett, Farmington, 1st.

White Crested Black Polish Hens—E. A. Drinkwater, 1st on fowl and 1st on chicks.

Silver Spangled Polish—S. Ward, 1st on fowls.

Buff Laced Polish—E. A. Drinkwater, 1st.

Silver Bearded Polish—Parker & Scripture, 1st and 2d on chicks; E. A. Drinkwater, 3d on chicks; S. Ward, 1st on fowl; E. A. Drinkwater, 2d on fowl.

TURKEYS.

Bronze—E. A. Drinkwater, 2d; M. F. Burnham, 3d.

Narragansett—A. J. Kenniston, 1st and 2d.

White—S. Ward, 1st.

Slate—A. J. Kenniston, 1st.

GEESE.

Toulouse—S. Ward, 1st and 3d; A. J. Kenniston, 2d.

Embden—A. J. Kenniston, 1st and 2d.

Brown China—M. F. Burnham, 1st and 2d; S. Ward, 3d.

Rouen Ducks—E. A. Drinkwater, 1st; Cayuga, A. J. Kenniston, Hermon Center, 1st; S. Ward, 2d; A. J. Kenniston, 3d; Aylesbury, A. J. Kenniston, 1st and 2d; S. Ward, 3d; Muscovy, colored, S. Ward, 1st; A. J. Kenniston, 2d; white, A. J. Kenniston, 1st and 2d; Pekin, E. A. Drinkwater, 1st; David McKnight, Lewiston, 2d; Parker & Scripture, 3d; White Call, A. J. Kenniston, 1st and 2d; E. A. Drinkwater, 3d; White Crested, S. Ward, 1st and 2d; Indian Runner, E. A. Drinkwater, 1st.

"From Maine to California."

We have received many compliments upon the appearance of our paper, and present a few of them here.

"I like the new name of your paper. It is well gotten up, just the right size, and full of solid stuff that I should think all practical workers would like."

F. O. WELLCOME, Yarmouth, Me.

"I think your last issue is a great improvement over the others. Advertising in your paper is money well invested."

H. W. GUNSTON, Groveland, Mass.

"Your paper is all right and deserves a wide circulation."

L. A. PRESBY, Sec., Malden Poultry Association, Malden, Mass.

"I think the change of name and purpose of the paper is a happy one. It is better than before, if that were possible. I speak a good word for the paper to all poultry people I know East or West."

MRS. E. I. COLE, Corning, Cal.

When the yards are covered with snow and the egg yield is low there is nothing that can equal cut clover as a base for the morning mash. It will increase the egg yield and also assist in making them more fertile. The best brand of cut clover on the market is prepared at Niagara Farm, W. R. Curtiss & Co., Props., Ransomville, N. Y. This farm produces annually from 15,000 to 20,00 Pekin Ducks, and large numbers of White Wyandottes. Belgian Hares are also bred quite extensively. They also carry a large line of incubators, bone cutters and poultry supplies of all kinds. This firm is perfectly reliable and trustworthy, and will be pleased to send circulars to the readers of this paper.

THE EASTERN POULTRYMAN.

SOUTH FREEPORT, MAINE.

Geo. P. Coffin,   -   Publisher.

Published the 1st of Each Month.
Subscription Price 25 Cents per Year.

OCTOBER, 1901.

Change of Location.

Beginning with the November issue
the EASTERN POULTRYMAN will be mailed
from the post-office at *Freeport*, Maine,
instead of South Freeport, and all future
correspondence should be sent to that
address.

The Maine State Poultry and Pet Stock
Association is receiving some liberal
donations to be used for special premiums at the show to be held in Lewiston in December. The Governor of
Maine, Hon. John F. Hill, has donated
$50.00 as prizes to be awarded on dressed
poultry by Maine exhibitors. Maine is
surely setting the pace for some of the
other states to follow.

We are pleased to announce that Mr.
J. W. Morse is to be a regular contributor
to the EASTERN POULTRYMAN for the
coming year. Mr. Morse has had thirty
years' experience in breeding thorough-
bred poultry for fancy and practical purposes, and has an entertaining way of
telling some of the things he has learned
from his own experience. His first article appears in this issue. In the November number will be an account of the
methods of work on a farm where a nice
profit is made from the poultry, and a
later paper will give an interesting account of a farm managed by two sisters
who have made a living from poultry
bred on fancy lines. We have some good
things in store for our readers.

In the poultry literature of to-day we
see a great improvement over that of ten
or twenty years ago. The tendency is
more and more to the practical methods,
and the best writers of to-day are those
whose knowledge has been gained by
actual experience, or who have actually
applied the facts gained by study, and
demonstrated the feasibility of methods
which were founded upon a sound
theory.

Many of the older poultrymen remember a Connecticut editor whose paper
and books written by him were filled with
ideas that appeared well theoretically,
but a farm conducted on the plans set
forth, could not succeed. The Utopian
schemes and impractical ideas of the past
are continually giving way to the broader
views, intelligent study and practical
application of the laws of breeding and
systems of management that are in vogue
upon the successful American poultry
farms.

One of our subscribers, in a personal
letter to the editor, refers to the literature
of the past and present as follows: " As
I look back upon the experience of my
few years of poultry keeping, the wrong
ideas, the impractical theories and methods that I absorbed from the poultry
papers seem to stand out more clearly
than anything else.

"This was no doubt due to an incorrect
conception on my part of the things they
sought to teach, but it certainly is not
easy for experience to fully realize the
perplexities of inexperience. At the
present time the competition in poultry
literature seems to be acting as a healthy
stimulant, and it seems to me that there
is more good sound sense being published in the journals than ever. I think
the symposium questions are interesting
and valuable. If a general interest could
be aroused so the readers would ask
questions and also answer the questions
of others it would be more interesting
than it is now. It seems as if by far the
greater part of the readers do not avail
themselves of the opportunity, especially
that of answering questions. They seem
to depend upon the editor for that.

"A sort of friendly 'give and take'
would certainly be interesting and would
undoubtedly bring out some good things,
and would emphasize facts in such a way
that the novice would the more readily
understand them."

To our mind, this feature of poultry
journalism should not be overlooked,
and the monthly experience meeting can
be made of great value to all. The great
trouble seems to be that each journal has
a small family that do all the writing.
Cannot this family be enlarged so that
each reader will feel perfectly free to ask
or answer the questions? Would not a
few pages of such matter be preferable
to the same amount of heavy theory on
the visionary views of "Thomas Incog-
nito, F. R. Z. S.," or Prof. Nemo, of the
Patagonia Experiment Station?

It is not our disposition to criticise the
work of the editors, or the contents of
our contemporaries, but that errors exist
must be plain to all readers. One of our
readers, a careful and thorough student
of poultry culture, writes us concerning
some misleading paragraphs that recently
appeared in two of our exchanges that
are usually carefully edited. He says:
" On page 148 of the current issue of the
Poultry Keeper we find the following:

" ' If there are a dozen hens in a yard
and the owner gets only six eggs a day
it is plain six of them are not laying.'
' Now a hen that produces an egg certainly requires more than a non-layer,' *
* * * 'All hens or pullets with red
combs should therefore be to themselves
and should be fed more than the non-
layers.' (Italics mine of course.)
"Is this not a remarkable statement
taken in whole or in part? What conclu-
sion will the novice seeking for light
arrive at from such a statement? The
flock of twelve hens laying an average of
six eggs per day are yielding 50 per cent,
and *every hen* may be laying.

"As a general proposition the laying
hens require more food than non-layers,
yet it by no means follows that *all* of the
non-layers in a flock are *always* over-fed.
Some of them may not be active enough
to get their share and hence do not lay
because *underfed.*

"In penning my non-layers separately
and feeding heavily on corn to prepare
for market I have very frequently had a
number of them begin laying and lay
fairly well for weeks.

"Now for the red combs. The natural
inference from that statement is that the
red combs are a sure indication that those
birds were laying and should be fed
accordingly. Several years ago I read a
similar statement and fed two pens of
pullets heavily with the result that I got
hardly an egg all winter, yet they were
healthy and happy and their bright scar-
let combs were a pleasure to behold.

"Leaving the red comb out of the
question altogether, the surest proof, if
you please the only proof that a hen is a
laying hen is the fact, shown by her eggs,
that she is laying.

"These things are of vital importance
to the beginner and it seems to me that
there can be no doubt that he often gets
no eggs because he incorrectly feeds the
healthy, happy, *red combed* hens or pullets at a time when egg production is a
matter of hopeful expectancy rather than
present attainment.

"In *A Few Hens* for September, page
27, under the caption 'Eggs and Egg
Farming,' we find this: 'All the egg foods
in creation won't make the hen lay when
she has stopped for moulting.' A literal
application of this wild statement would
doubtless prove it true. But let us take
it as it means and not as it reads.

"I have fifty-six hens that are all laying
and yielding from thirty to thirty-six eggs
a day now (the last of September). Most

of them are in moult and some of them have been since July. A number of the moulting hens have stopped laying and a change in the ration has started them again. Moulting hens as a rule do not lay unless carefully and wisely fed and cared for, but that does not warrant such a radical statement as the one quoted."

Brothers Jacobs and Boyer must be careful in the statements they allow to creep into their papers—but we are pleased to notice that these occurences are few and far between.

The Practical Questions of the Day are open for discussion and suggestions, and we trust that all our readers are interested in the practical knowledge that can be disseminated by this means. We make the invitation general for all to ask or answer. If writers prefer that their names be not published, please mention it.

A Poultry Visit.

It is always a pleasure for us to visit a poultry fancier who understands his work. Such a breeder is Prof. E. E. Peacock, of Kent's Hill, Maine, whose Barred Plymouth Rocks are quite well known among eastern fanciers.

While attending the Kennebec County Fair at Readfield, the poultry department of which was under Mr. Peacock's care, we accepted his invitation to visit his home, and were pleasantly entertained by Mr. and Mrs. Peacock.

The breeding of first-class Barred Plymouth Rocks is Mr. Peacock's particular hobby and that he understands it pretty well is evidenced by his winning at the Maine State Fair and Amesbury, Mass., Poultry Show in 1900.

His young stock was out on farms several miles distant, and we were unable to see them, but such of the old stock as we handled, including that on exhibition at Readfield (1st and 2d prize winners) showed that his line of cockerel breeders was especially strong. The males and females of this cockerel line are from the same stock that has produced many of the New York winners. He is also establishing a pullet line of good promise, and we confidently expect to see some of his stock take a high rank in the winter shows. He is also starting a nice flock of White Wyandottes which have already made a good record from a utility standpoint and are well up in the standard requirements. We can cheerfully recommend Mr. Peacock as a breeder whose stock and dealings will be found as represented.

In company with Mr. Peacock we called at the home of Mr. Webb Donnell, Kent's Hill, who is a fancier of several varieties, and had the pleasure of examining some of his Barred Plymouth Rocks, Brown Leghorns, Silver and Golden Seabright Bantams and Partridge Wyandottes. He also breeds pigeons and Angora rabbits. Mr. Donnell is engaged in literary work and the poultry is something of a side line, but is of such quality as would surely command respect in any show room.

"The EASTERN POULTRYMAN, published at South Freeport, Maine, is the new name for the *Poultryman and Pomologist*. Mr. George P. Coffin is editor and publisher. To judge by the September number, the new comer is a decided acquisition to the poultry literature of the United States."—*From the American Fancier (Johnstown, N. Y.), Sept. 28, '01*·

PRACTICAL QUESTIONS OF THE DAY.

In order to keep our paper in closest touch with its thousands of readers who are engaged in the work to which it is devoted, our aim is to have the readers express their ideas and the results of their own experience and observation concerning some of the subjects under discussion.

We shall publish each month a list of practical questions and invite our readers, one and all, to contribute their answers to any and all questions.

These answers will be published in the second paper after the question, and we shall hope for a full and free discussion. Our readers are also invited to ask any question of general importance. Perhaps the problem which is puzzling you may have been solved already by some of our readers, and the correct solution will help others as well as yourself. Then let the questions be forthcoming, and give us your answer to those asked by others. The EASTERN POULTRYMAN is published in your interests, and we invite you to join with us in improving its quality and extending its influence.

In sending answers we want not only the "yes" or "no," but we want the "how" and the "why," the "which" and the "when."

QUESTIONS TO BE ANSWERED IN THE DECEMBER NUMBER.

Is it advisable to promptly "break up" broody hens, and what is the best method of caring for them?

Is there any advantage in crossing breeds?

How many fowls can one man properly care for, raising chicks enough to replace the fowls disposed of each year, and keeping the stock in the best condition for profit?

How many fowls can profitably be kept on an acre?

What is the best method of caring for and using the poultry droppings?

Of what does your mash consist and at what time is it fed?

Rhode Island Reds and the American Standard.

Editor Eastern Poultryman:—

I notice in your September number a communication from Robert S. Taylor of Michigan, concerning the admission of the Rhode Island Reds to the American Standard of Perfection.

I have awaited with considerable interest to see what action the Committee of the Rhode Island Club would take regarding Mr. Taylor's request in "*Farm Poultry*," that a statement of the position of the Club on the question of admission to the standard be made. As this does not seem to be forthcoming, I think it only fair to our Western brothers to give them some indication, as an individual, of what I find to be the prevailing sentiment among the Eastern Red men.

I am very much interested in the Rhode Island Reds, and think I have some of the best in the country upon my farm. The steady progress of the breed toward that perfection, which I have seen attained in individual instances, is what I most desire, and anything which serves to hasten this progress has my hearty support. The question of admission to the standard, however, is an open one. Personally, I do not see how admission to any standard can improve the chances of the Rhode Island Red. I do not wish this to be taken as in any way casting reflection upon the American Standard of Perfection. The point I wish to make is, that the market for Reds is so good at present, and the interest in them is so great, that I do not think they need any stimulus in the way of admission to any standard but the one the Club adopts as its own, to enable them to achieve all the success that the most enthusiastic admirer could wish. Success with the fancier at large is measured by the market value of the birds. We may get as much pleasure as we like from the study of them in our own yards, and may breed purely for the sentiment of the matter; but the ultimate test of the success of the breed is the ability of the promoters to sell for fancy prices. However the situation may be in Michigan, certainly the prices demanded and secured during the last season for Rhode Island Reds — whether birds or fancy stock — were as large as is often paid for the best birds of any breed. The only fear I have for the Rhode Island Red is that it may move too fast. Whether admitting to the American standard would assist in the rapidity of rise in favor, I am not sure, but I do feel sure that such admission is not necessary at present to enable the breeders of good birds to obtain all they are fairly entitled to in the shape of cash returns for their better specimens, and from indications about here, I think there should be no complaint of the prices obtained for strictly utility birds.

There seems to be a fear in various quarters that there will be considerable opposition when the attempt is made to have the Reds admitted to the standard. The old story of confliction with Buff Plymouth Rocks and Buff Wyandottes need not be repeated here. Of one thing I am sure: those of us who are breeding and like our single Rose-Comb birds do not propose to give them up for the sake of having a Pea-Comb admitted to the standard. I believe there are distinctive features enough about the Rhode Island Red to prevent his ever being confounded with a Buff Plymouth Rock or a Buff Wyandotte, and if he cannot sail under his own colors, side by side with the other two breeds, I say let him go it alone. He has done it successfully so far in New England, and I believe is fully able to do so in the future. It is rather a remarkable fact that I have not met a Red breeder in New England in the past six months who has not expressed himself pretty much as I do, and I have talked with some of the best of them. I spent a whole day in the neighborhood where the standard Rhode Island Reds originated, driving about the country with one of the best recognized judges of Reds, and talking with the breeders of nearly all the best birds that have been shown in this part of the country, and without exception found them entirely indifferent on the question of admission to the standard, but apparently deeply imbued with the characteristics of the Rhode Island Red for putting up a stiff fight for supremacy wherever he meets a rival.'—There is more good solid kick to the Rhode Island Red fraternity than to any other aggregation of poultrymen, it has ever been my pleasure to meet.

I like the way. Mr. Taylor puts things, and especially commend the last paragraph of his letter to the perusal of the Rhode Island fraternity. It is almost impossible to prevent personalities creeping into business transactions. It seems to me that the way to do good work on the Rhode Island Reds is to keep whacking away at a standard of our own within the Club, trimming off a little here : adding a little there from time to time, and bringing the standard as near perfection as the individual desires, or the members of the Club will permit. Until we can arrive a good deal closer to an agreement within our own ranks as to what a male and female should both be like, it seems to me next to useless to make any particular effort to be admitted to the American Standard even if such admission could benefit the breed, which I doubt. For one, I should like to shake hands with Mr. Taylor and all his Western friends who are interested in this breed. Red men should certainly find a way to hang together within their own ranks, and I should very much deplore any action on the part of either the East or the West that should set the two sections at odds with each other. It is natural that the East should consider itself entitled to first recognition in all matters pertaining to this breed, as the East produced it, pushed it and intends to fight for it; but because this is so, is no reason why those interested in all sections of the country should not have part of the say-so as to what shall ultimately be done with it.

The above is written merely with an idea of giving Mr. Taylor a direct answer to his question from one who — in an individual capacity — has travelled over considerable of the Eastern country and talked with a great many breeders of Rhode Island Reds. What the Committee will report, I do not know. If Mr. Taylor can get any pointers out of this letter that will help him understand the situation, I shall be fully repaid for writing it.

Yours very truly,
THOMAS HOLLIS.
French Farm, Concord, Mass.

Rhode Island Reds and the "Standard."

Editor Eastern Poultryman:—

I was much interested in the communication of Mr. Robt. S. Taylor, in your issue of September, in relation to admitting Rhode Island Reds to the American Standard of Perfection. This is not the first article of a like nature that I have read by any means, but strange to say they all come from parties that are ignorant of the situation regarding this breed. If our good brother could have been present and taken part in the formation of the Rhode Island Red Club at Fall River, Mass., in 1898, he would have understood that it was the unanimous expression of breeders the present, that the last thing to be desired for this breed was its admission to the "Standard;" these gentlemen were thoroughly conversant with the composite make-up of the birds as bred by different parties and fully realized the vast amount of time and patience that would be required to finally evolve a breed that would breed reasonably true to color, and at the same time give satisfaction to the majority of breeders; and where could they receive

such careful attention and thoughtful consideration as in the hands of their friends? Surely not by putting them in the "Standard," for then the task of bringing order out of chaos, of finishing the crude material with which we started, into a thing of beauty, would have devolved upon parties who had no knowledge of their antecedents.

No, Mr. Editor, the place to perfect a Standard for this breed, which I anticipate must take a number of years yet, is in the hands of the gentlemen composing the "Rhode Island Red Club," and not that of the American Poultry Association.

The breed has already been recognized by the leading poultry associations of the country, such as Boston, New York, Philadelphia, etc., and I know of none of the smaller associations in the east that have not given it a place in their catalogues.

The great importance that the various "Specialty Clubs" are now assuming in the poultry world bids fair to overshadow any action that the A. P. A. may take regarding the "Standard" to be put on any breed, and I think it is not expressing too optimistic an opinion to say that the time will come when all breeds of poultry will have their "Specialty Clubs" and when such a time does come, instead of the A. P. A. making the "Standards" for the different breeds, they will go to them for their ideas in such matters and will not dare to set up a "Standard" for any breed that has not first received the approval of the "Specialty Club" representing that breed.

Respectfully yours,
FRED B. COCHRAN.

Blood Will Tell.

Writers on this subject differ widely, which I believe is largely due to their personal prejudices ; and we doubtless read many articles where the writer tells of the remarkable success attained with a certain breed or variety, when, if the truth were known, it might prove to be the only breed ever kept by the writer. There are nevertheless certain facts that a person who has had experience with different breeds can explain, which are often of great benefit to those who are about to engage in the business and are uncertain as to what breed to select.

It has been the aim of the American fanciers to establish an all-purpose breed, and to a large extent their efforts have been crowned with success; yet, strictly speaking, the all-purpose fowl does not exist to-day. It should be the purpose of every true fancier to enlighten those who contemplate engaging in the business, yet there are doubtless a large number who are as much in the dark on this subject after reading the poultry papers as they were before they began to seek information through that source, for the reason that so many articles are misleading. A person naturally writes about the breed he is interested in, and I fear some overdo the matter. One person says, " The Barred Plymouth Rocks are the best all-purpose fowl and that they are good layers." Now, the beginner reasons that if they are "good layers," that is what he is after, so that he at once proceeds to stock a large egg farm with Barred Plymouth Rocks, only to find out at the end of a year or so that what he wanted was Leghorns; that he is producing flesh faster than eggs ; that he might have had more eggs and larger eggs at much less cost.

Another person wants to start a broiler plant, and he reads that Leghorns are much used as broilers in New York City.

He finds that when he begins to market his product in a northern market that they are not in demand ; that those who have plump Wyandottes or Plymouth Rocks receive the highest price because they reach that desirable 1½ to 2 pounds weight sooner than the Leghorn.

The Standard of to-day shows a classification of ten breeds of fowls, as follows: American, Asiatic, Mediterranean, Polish, Hamburg, French, English, Games, and a miscellaneous class which includes six other breeds, and I think they are classed very much in the order of their popularity. The writer of these notes has been a close observer, and has had many years' experience in breeding most of the popular varieties, largely of the first named breeds,—namely, the American, Asiatics, and Mediterranean, and I will briefly describe them (as breeds) as I have found them.

All unbiased breeders will, I think, admit that among the American breeds will be found the best varieties for meat. They are the most popular in most markets. They are very hardy, and enormous eaters, which very traits fit them for the purpose in which they excel, making them available at any age for market. They can be made to weigh one and one-half pounds at nine weeks of age. (The writer speaks from experience, as he marketed May 1, several dozen Barred Plymouth Rocks at that age, some of the largest weighing just two pounds each). It will therefore be seen that the American breeds excel as a market fowl, and their strong points are against them when kept for other purposes.

The Mediterraneans will naturally lay more eggs in a year than any other breed and I believe on less feed. The cost of raising them to the age of laying is much less than the American breeds, and with proper care and housing will, in my opinion, excel even them as winter layers. They are then the breed for the egg farm, and as there are twelve varieties of this breed one should certainly be suited as to color and type.

The Asiatics are to-day, and always have been, popular. They can be depended upon for eggs in winter. It has been my experience that they will pay much better during the extreme cold months than either of the above named breeds. Their eggs are large and of a color that makes them popular in certain markets, yet they cannot compete with the first two named breeds in the race for favor as the producer of meat or eggs. Then why their popularity ? Because they are the fowl for the farm ; they command the highest prices in the show room. The first prize Buff Cochin cockerel at New York in 1895 sold for $250. No one will deny that the Asiatics excite their share of admiration in the show room. There is no fowl more capable of being shown. Why should not a person pause before a pen containing a Black Langshan cockerel of the correct type, to admire that much sought after tail carried at just the right angle to make the profile of back " just about right," or that Light Brahma cock as he stands there clothed in spotless white ; set off with a jet black tail and perfect neck, tipping the beam at fourteen pounds ? Why that crowd in front of the pen containing the first prize Buff Cochin pullet —one mass of beautiful soft feathers molded into graceful outlines ? What a wonderful combination of form and color ? Is it strange that such specimens command good prices ?—*Michigan Poultry Breeder.*

DANGER FOR RHODE ISLAND REDS.

Continued from Page 22.

counteract the females' color, or bought again specifying that they receive very dark red females. This general demand for very dark birds causes breeders to breed them darker and darker (a chocolate or chestnut color) much darker than is natural and much darker than is desirable, I believe. Had no birds bred to buff standard been sold as Reds, and all buyers been informed that males and females ought not to match in color, no such radical change would have taken place. Had there been no Buff Rocks or Wyandottes made from Red stock, breeders would not·have been forced to breed as they have, and there would have been no. question about whether Reds should be admitted to the American Standard.

With the causes understood, the natural difference between the male and female fully recognized, and the standard built accordingly, the danger of breeding to an undesirable, extreme color, that would lessen the attractiveness of the male, or cause fanciers to adopt double matings to produce show birds that will match, can be avoided. I hope this will be done eventually. That it is desirable to make the females redder than their original color, I believe, but it should be done by deepening and brightening the natural colors, rather than by changing the color and doing away with the contrast between upper and lower portions of the body. The most attractive females I have ever. seen, those that showed the brightest and most lively colors, and that faded least at any season or when old, had bright red necks with lighter breasts and other parts, the neck being darkest and gradually shading off to other portions. This sort of color would, probably, in breeding, also help in securing the desired color in the males' hackle. When the first Rhode Island Red Club Standard was formed, the tendency to breed out the black in females' hackle was corrected by requiring a slight amount of black in hackle. The last revision at Boston leaves out "slight," therefore calls for more distinct black. These markings black in hackle and tail that standard now calls for, with this deep red in neck, are natural markings, and would sufficiently distinguish the females from the buff breeds, and there would be no call for breeding the whole body one dark, even color, which some fancier judges are doing their best to encourage.

LOSS OF PRESTIGE AS DRESSED POULTRY.

Among the improved Reds, as now bred, may still be found many different types. Some are bred of Leghorn shape and weight, having similar nervous organization and high tails, slender upright bodies, slender necks, and legs, and with great tendency to white earlobes. These are distinctly of the egg-type, and while they, like Leghorns, make good small broilers, they are hard to fatten when older, and are not of much account as dressed chickens or fowl. Other types can hardly be told from Wyandottes in shape, and a type very much. like the Plymouth Rock is seen. Other strains resemble Langshans and Cochins in shape and general carriage and weight. They lay rich tinted eggs, are very hardy and heavy when dressed. It has lately gone out from certain quarters, from not entirely disinterested parties, that Rhode Island Reds are not satisfactory dressed poultry, that they belong to the egg class and are not an all-purpose fowl: This is certainly true if you judge them by the Leghorn type; it is another matter if you judge them by the Wyandotte type or American Dominique type. Then you will not see much difference between them and Wyandottes, except they have longer bodies, not quite so long necks and legs, and are a little smaller and quicker to mature. Judging them by the ten and twelve-pound Cochin or Langshan type, they are solid as anything, good heavy-dressed poultry stock, just the thing for hardy winter chickens and roasters. It all depends upon the type you judge them by. I favor the type about between the Cochin and American Dominique; wider· and plumper than Plymouth Rocks and shorter on their legs. As plump as Wyandottes but longer in body and wider in the back, not quite so coarse in form or long in neck or legs. Not quite so square and low on legs as Dorkings. The new standard adopted at last Boston show contains nothing different from the old one in regard to type. It calls for the shape peculiar to varieties of the American class, and a long keel. Specifies that Rock or Wyandotte shape is not required.

No breed of the American class does or should carry body upright, or has large tails or carries them high. The Leghorn type is certainly not called for. When the judge who has lately placed awards on Reds at Boston looks the birds over he generally compares their body to an oblong card. This shows his idea of outline shape. He has an ideal that the accepted standard hardly hints at. Why should this ideal be kept secret? Why not express it in the standard and then tie judges down to it? Same with all other fine points. Why not give breeders the country over the same chance to breed to the highest ideals that those who meet this judge personally have? Is it desirable to have a wide-open, easy standard published, that will not prevent the sale of low grade Reds for good ones, and an unwritten one that is known to few, but in reality governs judges and experienced breeders and exhibitors? — *Samuel Cushman in June and July Poultry Monthly, 1901.*

Short Talk on Feeds.

It seems reasonable that we should pay particular attention to what we feed our poultry, for unless we feed it properly it cannot become profitable. Take the case of a laying hen for instance. If we only feed her enough to merely keep her in good health she cannot produce eggs, as she must have material from which to make eggs before she can produce them. In order to keep alive and in good health a hen must have a certain amount of feed. This feed must contain all the elements that go to make up her body and certain other elements that furnish the motive power to keep her going, for it is well understood that the mere condition of existing requires feed to support life. It is all very simple. The feed is taken into the stomach and in that wonderful organ is changed by chemical action, or rather is resolved into its original elements and these are used according to the needs of the body. A part of the feed goes to keep up the temperature of the body, keep life going and give power to live, breathe and move. This power is called vital energy and is kept going by consuming a part of the feed taken into the stomach, just the same as steam is kept in a steam engine by burning fuel under the boiler. The feed is fuel, to that extent. For this purpose the oils, fats, gums, sugar and other similar elements that are in the feed are used. These are collectively spoken of as the carbohydrates. There is another element that is absolutely necessary. This is the albuminous portion of the feed and is called protein. Protein goes to the building up of the nerves, bones, muscles—lean meat—tendons, brain, arteries, veins and feathers. The white of an egg is albumen, in its purest state, and water. The fact that eggs are so largely composed of albumen, which comes from the protein of the feed they eat, shows the necessity of feeding those feeds that are rich in protein. If we feed corn, which has a large amount of the carbohydrates and but little albumen, the hen gets too much of the carbohydrates, and when this is the case, the surplus is stored up in the body as fat. This explains why a fat animal or fowl that is deprived of feed grows poor. The fat is then used to keep up vitality, being consumed in the body exactly as feed is and for the same purpose, except that fat can never become protein.

This should be understood: Fat can never take the place of protein, nor can the carbohydrates be used to make those parts of the body that are made of protein, but in the absence of a sufficient quantity of the carbohydrates protein is used in its place. As protein is the costliest of the necessary elements of feed it is not good economy to feed an insufficient quantity of the carbohydrates.

This brings up the question of a balanced ration. This is a ration that contains enough of the carbohydrates to furnish vital energy and enough protein to keep the muscles, bones, brain and nerves in repair. In animals this would require about one part of protein to five or six of the carbohydrates. A cow giving milk, which is rich in albuman, or a laying hen, requires much more protein than this ration calls for. In the case of a laying hen she must not only have enough protein to keep her body in good working order, but she must have enough extra to supply the large amount of albumen in the eggs she produces. This being true, we must study how we can supply her with this protein at the lowest cost. Fresh meat is rich in protein, but it costs too much. Fresh cut bones furnish protein, as well as some fat, and lime for egg-shells, but it is not always possible to get them. Meat meal, ground beef scraps and dried blood are very rich in protein and the laying hen fed either of these will extract from them enough albumen to supply all the material for as many eggs as she can produce. These feeds are always available as they can be kept in any climate any length of time and remain sweet, pure and wholesome.

Wheat, oats, bran, middlings and gluten meal are all rich in protein and should be liberally used in feeding laying hens or growing poultry, but none of them can take the place of green cut bones or some of the dried and ground preparations of beef. It is not saying too much to say that one of these is absolutely necessary to the greatest success.

Milk, in any form, sweet, sour or buttermilk, is rich in albumen, but this is so largely diluted with water that hens cannot get enough of the albumen in the quantity of milk they can consume.

As a drink it is a valuable addition to the amount of protein that can be got into what a hen consumes, but it lacks in quantity.

For young poultry, where we must have material to build the frame, as bones, muscles, nerves, etc., we must feed large quantities of protein, and its cheapest form is in the shape of one of the meat preparations. The cost is low—about 2 cents a pound, and less in quantities—and no poultry breeder, no matter where he lives, can afford to do without this form of feed. The only reason why hens lay better in summer than in winter is because they keep warm and comfortable and get large quantities of protein in the bugs, worms and other forms of animal feed they find by foraging. We can keep hens warm in winter quite easily. The only other thing necessary is animal feed, and we can get this cheaply in green cut bones or animal meal.—*Commercial Poultry.*

An Industry with Many Branches.

When we who profess to be poultrymen speak of some people who know little of our profession, we sometimes get the retort, "Oh, the poultry business don't amount to anything, any fool can throw out a grain to a flock of birds two or three times a day." Such is their vague idea of the amount of care our birds require, and many go into the business with as little knowledge of its requirements, and usually give up in disgust as soon as they begin to get a little experience. Lately I have corresponded with two parties; both have hired others to take charge of their poultry. One makes the assertion that the business is one continual expense, and the other one wanted to hire another poultryman but was not willing to give what would be reasonable wages to an experienced man. Both have exceptionally good home markets, but I doubt if their poultry business will amount to anything until they are willing to pay more than ordinary farm hand wages to their poultrymen. Ordinary brawn is sufficient to do farm work, but it takes more than ordinary brains to make a successful poultryman, and brains are worth more on the market than brawn.

A poultryman must plan his work months ahead, and have system and management in his work if his business is of any extent. How many of us have ever stopped to think over the numerous branches connected with the business?

Here is a list of what a poultryman keeping only fowls may have for sale:

1. Eggs for market.
2. Eggs for hatching.
3. Newly hatched chicks.
4. Weaned chicks.
5. Squab broilers.
6. Broilers.
7. Fries.
8. Small roasters.
9. Large roasters.
10. Capons.
11. Young stock for breeders.
12. Old breeding stock.
13. Feathers.
14. Manure.

There are 14 different products that one could raise from a single pen of fowls. Most of these articles would apply to other domesticated birds that a poultryman might keep—ducks, geese, turkeys, pigeons, bantams and guineas So we see he might have over 50 products to dispose of and still be exclusively a poultryman, and have but one breed of each species. But the probability is that he would not make a success with the 50 products, as his market might be one where even a third of those products could be disposed of at a profit. Right here is where many fail; they do not study their market.

It is each poultryman's first lookout to know what will sell best in his own market. Eggs usually sell well in our northern states, therefore many make a specialty of egg farming; some find it more profitable to turn the eggs into chicks. A few make a specialty of squab broilers, claiming that by marketing the birds when two months old they can get their money back quickly and start another lot. Others keep the birds until they get to broiler or market size, as they grow much faster after two months old, need no brooding, nor as expensive foods as at the start, and mortality is very slight after the second month. Still a few others caponize their cockerels and keep them for a year or more before sending them to market. There are numerous poultrymen who make a specialty of ducks, selling at ten weeks old. This was quite a profitable business near eastern cities five or ten years ago, but the ducklings being so easy to raise, many have gone into the business of late years and consequently prices have dropped considerably with an increased supply. Geese and turkeys are seldom made an exclusive business, but are profitable adjuncts to a poultry business where the owner has the proper facilities and understands handling them. Pigeons are very attractive to some, and squab raising is often quite remunerative if the right market is secured. Squabs usually bring one dollar more a dozen in the New York market than in Boston. We can see from this fact how a producer living midway between the two cities might make the difference between profit and loss by shipping squabs to New York instead of Boston.

We have not yet considered the fancy business. Eggs for hatching at two or more dollars a sitting looks like a "good thing" for the producer, but these eggs meet so often with mishaps that spoil the hatches that it often hurts a man's trade, therefore many refuse to sell the eggs, preferring to set them all themselves rather than risk their reputation on something over which they have no control. I believe it is the opinion of the majority of breeders that it would be much to the satisfaction of both buyer and seller if the eggs for hatching business was done away with. Still this branch of the business seems to increase every year, and no doubt will still increase as long as the buyer sees the possibility of getting three or four good birds, as it would seem, for the price of one. From my own experience, both as a buyer and a seller, I think, as I said before, dealing in the mature stock to be more satisfactory to both parties, as the buyer can see just what he is getting, while hatches from our best stock often turn out very poorly. Late in the breeding season most breeders have a limited number of old breeding birds that they will sell at a low figure because of their age. Often these birds can be bred for a few years longer and if discouraged from laying through the fall and winter they make good breeders in the spring when their eggs are wanted for hatching.

I almost forgot to speak of the byproducts of the poultry yard—feathers and manure. Although these products are often allowed to waste, if preserved and sold they add a neat little sum to a year's account. The writer has been able to sell feathers and manure to such advantage that in the course of a year they paid 10 per cent of the feed bills.

All the foregoing shows the number of different lines of work connected with a poultry business. Although a number of these are practised as an exclusive business, they are each dependent on some of the others, so usually there is more profit in combining a few of the more remunerative rather than have a specialty that only brings in cash during a part of the year. For instance, in egg farming there is very little coming in through the fall when birds are moulting, and often in winter the weather will be such as to reduce the egg production. If raising roosters is combined with the egg farming they can be marketed just at a season when the eggs are scarce, killing the cockerels and saving pullets for layers. If the person with this combination has pure bred stock he may often be able to sell some of his best specimens at an advanced price and the same with eggs for sitting in the spring when there is always a large surplus and market prices very low. How nicely these different branches of the industry seem to fit in together; but remember, the remark will bear repetition, "It is each poultryman's first lookout to know what will sell best in his own market." That product must have first consideration and others come in as they are necessary or profitable.

In closing I should like to speak of another branch of the business, and that is raising birds for breeders who do an extensive business and are unable to raise the necessary number themselves. To a person of little means it is a fine opportunity, for he is usually very well paid for his labor and is not under any expense for advertising, nor need he worry about securing a market for his produce. I know of a breeder who gives parties eggs to set through the spring and in October takes all the better birds, paying $1.25 apiece for them, and the person raising them can dispose of the culls as he pleases, pocketing the proceeds. Of course, such instances are rare, but the man who keeps his eyes open and uses his brains is the one who will find just such chances and make the best of them.—*Poultry Success.*

Meeting of the American Buff Leghorn Club.

There will be a meeting of the American Buff Leghorn Club at the Pan-American Poultry Exhibition, at Buffalo, N. Y., Friday, Oct. 25, 1901, at 2 o'clock P. M. A large meeting is promised, and all persons interested in this popular fowl are requested to join the Club and be present. The Club offers a silver cup at the Pan-American, to be competed for by members only. Are you a member?

CHAS. H. THAYER, Pres.,
Chicago, Ill.
GEO. S. BARNES, Sec.,
Battle Creek, Mich.

Manchester, N. H., Poultry Association.

The 8th annual exhibition of the Manchester, N. H., Poultry Association will be held Jan. 21-24, 1902. N. H. Walker, Pres.; W. B. Sanford, Sec.; D. J. Lambert, C. A. Ballou, J. F. Watson, Judges.

"Congratulations and my ad herewith. Glad to see you come out 'clean shirted' for poultry only."
WM. C. KING, Homestead Poultry Farm, Hopkinton, Mass.

CPSIA information can be obtained
at www.ICGtesting.com
Printed in the USA
BVHW031225021118
531991BV00008B/818/P